I0760030

TABAKO ON THE WINDOWSILL

HARI ALLURI

ALSO BY
HARI ALLURI

The Flayed City
Carving Ashes

TABAKO ON THE WINDOWSILL

(POEMS TO BURN)

HARI ALLURI

BRICK BOOKS

Library and Archives Canada Cataloguing in Publication

Title: Tabako on the windowsill / Hari Alluri.
Names: Alluri, Hari, author.
Identifiers: Canadiana (print) 2024053378X | Canadiana (ebook) 2024053381X | ISBN 9781771316491 (softcover) | ISBN 9781771316507 (EPUB) | ISBN 9781771316514 (PDF)
Subjects: LCGFT: Poetry.
Classification: LCC PS8601.L553 T33 2025 | DDC C811/.6—dc23

We gratefully acknowledge the Canada Council for the Arts, the Government of Canada through the Canada Book Fund, and the Ontario Arts Council and the Government of Ontario for their support of our publishing program.

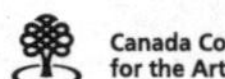

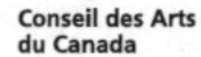

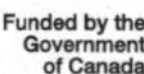

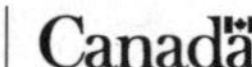

Edited by Chris Abani.
Author photo by Carlo Sayo.
The book is set in Athelas and Metallophile Sp8 with ornaments in Nymphette.
Design by Kilby Smith-McGregor.

Brick Books
487 King St. W.
Kingston, ON
K7L 2X7

www.brickbooks.ca

Though much of the work of Brick Books takes place on the ancestral lands of the Anishinaabeg, Haudenosaunee, Huron-Wendat, and Mississaugas of the Credit peoples, our editors, authors, and readers from many backgrounds are situated from coast to coast to coast in Canada on the traditional and unceded territories of over six hundred nations who have cared for Turtle Island from time immemorial. While living and working on these lands, we are committed to hearing and returning the rightful imaginative space to the poetries, songs, and stories that have been untold, under-told, wrongly told, and suppressed through colonization.

DEDICATED TO THE LIVING MEMORY
OF ERIC CARDENO, HOLLY KANG,
AND KAT ZU'COMULWAT NORRIS

CONTENTS

I.

II.

III.

We must know our loss, all things
that ghost our time.
Speak now, collect every bone,
lay the pieces together.

—Gémino H. Abad, "The Light in One's Blood"

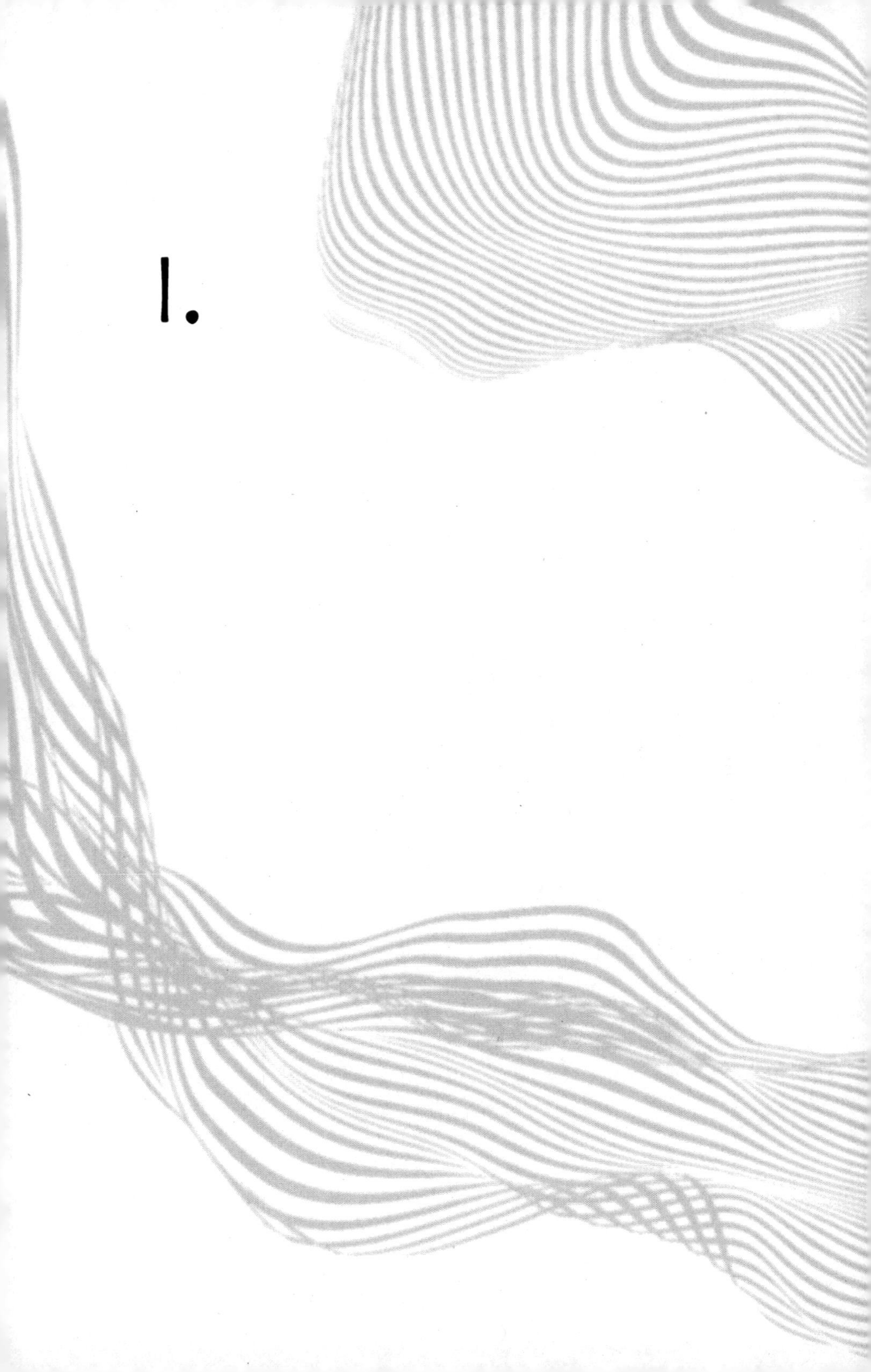

I.

The Cigarette Is Pretext: Smoke Rises from Within

Unless you're as practiced as a lola's wrinkles
do not flip the lit side of the yosi in your mouth.
They developed this skill in war and carried it
into supervised work with no breaks to speak of.
My smoking is less like revolution, but it helps on the job.
There's an extra few minutes of break-time for you, depending
on how slammed your co-workers are. Be generous:
ashtrays and pavements, what they have to take,
it won't come back half-nice. The kisses taste
exquisite as ash. Nods in the rain, friendships
you find and forget. The trick to becoming
a proper smoker is some small grief
there is no relief from and you know it,
so you might as well light something on fire
on a regular basis, take it in and breathe it out
like it's part of your everyday being. It's okay
if the grief is large. It's more important to find less
violent ways of spitting. The worst
way to spit is like a man who has sized up
another human being and is claiming to measure
their worth when he's really measuring his own
self-disdain. The worst way to smoke
is like you don't want to. I've felt it so many times
from people like me: we ask for a yosi, claiming
we've quit, or—more honest but not less painful—
lamenting we can't. Don't get me wrong,
pulling singles when you can't manage
the pack is fully acceptable. I'm only warning
against wistfulness. The smoke knows,
holds on for fear of being abandoned
as tight as you wish you were free. I would say I'm sorry but I
already told you smoke works like grief.
Don't need yellow-stained fingers to know this:

you could just burn the oil in the soup pot
by walking away while heating it up
and have to run it outside. Fingers scalding as you inhale
what's promised. You could just be sad
without the smoke for company. You could
call your lola's smoke-voice the first island
you're from. Keep the light, I have another right here.

Zoom Call with Lunar Moth on the Wall, and Tilting

I focus on the hallow around your face. Instead of all this missing, the planet your head makes, the giraffe of you because you hold your laptop camera down by your chest. I like when I mishear what you, or anyone, says. It's the mishearing that makes me awed by that small adjustment of meaning sound turns in my body—from translucent to ecstatic, irreversible as awe. When you show me how you did the magic trick, my awe still lingers. When I hurt at you reminding me how callous I have been to you, that undertow is only mine, cross-tiding my awe that you noticed anything I did. You notice things, maybe, like the earth notices them—not just the glint in a friend's eye when they're sexting; not like a camera panning and pulling and pushing closer—as something always already there. Like how I only learnt about the Goddess of Lost Things through that hazy, lazy, nasty, holy portal of the Google search and filled with awe that I could have found her after so long searching for any god to love me as I am. You remind me of siya: the genders you struggle in and declaim, whoever you miss wrapping arms around your name, you remind me of Anagolay because you know what losing is. Because you know what losing is, I diagnose you god: an entity who might love another as they are: a being who's lost, someone who, from the meanest deep, even if only because they're standing in the kitchen with the light behind them, has a hallow around their head. Fallow with want. Filling me with awe though I know the magic trick: you're in the kitchen somewhere else. I can't remember how you smell. It must be something like loss. It might be the thing that makes any of us holy.

Feel at How It's Etched

A single strand of spider's work
affixed to the bannister's
outside metal, if pointed
upward, almost vertical, by wind.

Maybe this is an altar too:
the cigarette whose seam I lick,
pull apart to the filter, roll
between thumb and finger to loosen
into my waiting palm. Place at the edge
where the bannister meets the muscle
memory in the web that's given up its maker
and inhabitant, the shape of its old life.

The water glass I whisper into, then sip.

A family of three locked into
our apartment tears at each other's seams,
can't seem to each make enough space
in this too-small home for the others'
wishes not to disappear. For my part, I ask
my love and child for nothing at first, which is
to hide from asking too much. I offer
more than I can give, then point at
what I couldn't give, demanding
it be offered. The dishes don't get
any cleaner the louder I clank them.

This is my hand, scooping
what gets caught in the sink's
nastier and nastier plastic
sieve. Let this feeling be only mine:
this restlessness in the morsels of food
stuck beyond saving, this slime of obligation

I finally embrace. Even exile
from that ease of aloneness
I used to take for granted
can be a form of freedom. I say this
only later, yosi smoke curling
off my fingertips to hold itself
to—and with—that strand it swirls
into a wave before dispersal.

Windowsill Offering to Anagolay, Goddess of Lost Things

I'm sorry, po, I've been frantic-search invoking you as I open up the freezer
praying, closer to first resort. Even before but especially since Mahal
called me over from its escaping frost, pointed to my missing phone, already cold to lift.

I keep on mistaking things that I misplace for actual loss:
my keys, my ciggy pack. I often joke that lighters, like socks,
should be considered among the class of interdimensional beings:

the way a pocket, checked three times and empty—when I shuck its jacket on
a weather cycle later, dig my right hand in for the pen I just put into it—
will press the lighter's body to my palm.

Especially since Apo shared how my mother's people carry you, Anagolay po,
as both creator and as the familiar who waits behind a tombstone:

I need a smaller god for this forgetfulness of mine.

On smaller days, a gift: I used to call
every clothing dryer your altar, the clean and fluffy
warm-touched single socks your pasalubong.

I had a Saint Anthony pendant for a while—
no doubt you've had to hide behind his name—but lost it, too.

You just have so much work to do, Deity of Lost Things, po. The lives
at your crossroads, the parts of land along with them, even if only the few I've loved.

Maybe if I—in danger of withering
your powers with this act—invented a deity of misplaced
objects and forgetfulness, no direct relationship
despite the life of lighters, to those
dimensional portals where you dwell.

My favourite Bulosan short story is an origin of tobacco, volcano god and all.
He made it up, and I know that where I am is where it's from: the medicine
isn't mine. What I can tell you is which corner stores sell my brand
cheaper when I buy packs in pairs. That story: I read it in an airport
and haven't seen the mountains of my mother's islands since, so it's a little like a home.

The thing that makes my offering of yosi leaf worth anything at all?
Because I want to keep it for myself.

So, because I feel somehow about calling out your name for my missing lighter
and for a missing beloved—someone's—a few breaths apart, I'm inventing that other deity.

And, because when it's government behind the disappearances, whoever knows too much
will be who's taken next, and those who remain wherever *here* might be for them
must make a semblance out of the partialities we have left.

Of course, when I say *Lola* I see wrinkled fingers, my lola's
one good ring. Say *marriage*, and there's a leather jacket, 70s lapels and blue,
left behind on a bus after an attempt to make up, me walking home in rain.

And today: one of those old blue tins for cigarettes,
with butt-out marks that refuse to wash completely off, but just
the rectangular outline shape of it, faded into the pocket of my jeans.

Here's somebody else's keys whose teeth haven't bit into a lock in years.
And here, my tiny oversized lamentations when I'm already running late
and step back through the apartment door yet another time—

calling out that made-up deity's name, while the reason you can find anything,
dear Anagolay, is simply because everything is tethered to your essence, po.

I'm worried at your diminishment and you're out there. Shaking your head
as if to say, *The smallest loss in all the world is worthy of my name.*

Windowsill Offering for My Nanay, with Help from Anagolay

Mama, here is the simplicity of it:
you birthed me between two harmattans. And the volcanic
arkipelago you are from is where you were still kneeling.
A C-section, a sickly child. Now a man, I cannot give you
the komiks you rented for the change you received
from your childhood market shopping
in town. Can't return you to those hours when
the deaths drawn in black-and-white ink
protected you from the question of your
soldier dad's return. Can't read any of it

but the pictures I've never seen. You would have
walked the miles back from town to village
instead of asking the driver for a ride, and one look
at the neighbour in the paddy hat told you
no chance of searching his basket for your last
coin that just fell in. You vowed to always
have at least a second coin in your pocket from then on.
You became a woman who would walk from any job
where the boss chanced you once too often.

Because I can never thank you for the all,
let me thank you for two small things: a love
of comic books; the creation shape of the Lingling-o
as a pendant on a necklace you don't remember
getting me. A type of coin I will never give over
without a fight. Filled with your embarrassment
and your hard-won voice, I live a life of digging
into that basket now—beneath the living fish and
heavy fruits, to reach the coin you dropped, worth
even less today, dull from so much years unspent
but true—. There at the weathered base of woven rattan.

Poem to Burn: **From Spiral and Storm**

The world this morning
reminds me too much
of my insides

that night I almost
abandoned the balcony.
Three pages deep of furious

language. Scratching
worry into my journal
before I can say, *please,*

let me—

on the outside table
this jagged bouquet:

tobacco seeds, dried,
still attached to the cut
few inches of their last-year stalks,

wrinkled fire
in a mini vase. It doesn't look much
like promise, but it is.

Windowsill Offering for Mahal

When I sent you a photo of two cards, the two
that felt safe to send, I said it was to not assume

our linking in the third. To not put pressure on you.
I lied. I didn't tell you I was on a rooftop patio

trying to quell my want with drink. Wishing I was
with you in Chicago when you picked up

the lid of that clay vessel with the tattoo etchings,
which was the first photo you sent me that made

my eyes water. I said I was protecting you from my desire.
As if a residence for spirits who multiply the rice

could be made from anything without that. You know,
I was protecting myself by not giving you the option

to respond with just your truth. *A reunion of two souls*
re-learning our own power—that's what you said to me.

So, thanks to you, here is a photo of all three cards,
with the third, which was the middle card,

unhidden. Varuna, Kilaka, Ganesha
mudras. Two water, one fire. May I share with you

my truth, knowing that every time I do, you might—
and this is scarier—you might just choose to choose me as I am.

When I Walk in She's Mixing Someone's Drink, Hitting the Notes on "How Will I Know," and Later We Together-Laugh at an Inside Joke on Us

Tita bartender, LAX, tuxedo
behind a name plate. Three songs deep she drops

into whichever hook comes on
while wide-eyeing a customer around this U-shape bar.

Now, Lisa Lisa & Cult Jam so—to each other—we sing
lost in emo-shuh-hunnn

and I know why I pulled up on this stool
after getting through: the special coded

light that signals random check; dimensions of
the stare I met before it blinked to stop me; the classic

break I battled to in my head, back-
talking the gloves up in my stuff,

catchy, stretched out. I sat down here to feel a distance,
the distance in bodies who recognize

belonging feels like someone else's music.
Que sera que sera

over top of the next song's bridge
bends the language that suppressed our tongues

333 years: she makes it
more beautiful. I'm dancing in my seat.

Origin Story

No boat, the Goddess of Lost Things,
no container for my seeking. I'm sorry
I didn't know my nanay's people had another
name for Anagolay—please allow my previous
invented version: how siya came to be (there's a river in this story;
I don't know where to put it). Let's say, in the beginning,
there was pure consciousness,
then jump to here, now a city,
in the green space between this mall's parking lot and
those apartments, facing the wound
in the trunk of this blighted cherry tree, larger than your torso,
shaped like an open human pelvis heart, a serrated
landscaper's blade in the innermost fold
camouflaged against the healing scar.
Behind you, around that lone cedar, the sunfire and white rose
petals fade into the ground. When they do,
whoever keeps leaving them here will no doubt bring more.

You might wonder how
somebody could have died in this place
but you're not thinking how this city came to be,
are only thinking that this is the earth,
whose every inch is rich in death's memory
and so you smile
at the thought of lining the planet's
entire surface with petals,
at the joyous grief that all will fade, the simple fact
that the act is nothing this world hasn't already
been doing since the first petal changed its colour
and you recall instead the sparkling
sunset through a beer glass
when your friend warned you that if you lose yourself
in any one story, even a true one,
eventually you lose that story as well.

There, in the mall lot to your right, two cars
used to pull up next to each other after close,
one driver getting out and joining the other.
I do not want my own desires to choose the make and model,
the drivers' genders and styles of dress.
What I know is this: they kiss and then relent.
Then one evening, when no more lies that matter remain
between them, they walk over to that patch of grass,
hand in hand. Each releases
petals onto the ground beside the cedar tree.
They make love, awash in shadows
thrown by the cherry tree's branches
under that street lamp's light in wind.
It is the most beautiful lovemaking of either's life.
They cry, feeling themselves close to returning
to the memory of themselves before bodies were invented.
Here is the summation of their loss:
a sock-patch needle, an empty trunk, a tired deck of cards.
The one who is left behind returns to this place,
lays down among petals the way the two used to,
imagines the other's body close at hand
into release, does so each night
till the petals are faded, offers once more,
returns home to sacrifice the only life acceptable.
The rose colours fade and no one comes to replace them.

If you arrive upon this story, petals appear behind you
to fade again. Someone has touched hands at the holy ground,
which could be any ground, ancient and brand new
grass, chopped up gravel, river bed.
Now you turn to surrender the story,
knowing what we all know, that you must surrender it
before surrendering to it, the way
what was alone sacrificed aloneness itself

in favour of a universe of bodies
moving in relation, demanding my people
encounter, then invent, a goddess of lost things.

Threshold Offering for Crossroads That Keep on Forming

We look; we're still looking.
—David Maduli, "Microclimates"

I'm carrying the fact of it, another ending.
I tell this to you on our way here, paré, so it
doesn't weigh down the work we came to do.
This spot, shaded by an evergreen so large
if it were hollow, we could have parked inside
its trunk. Older, you say, than the rounds of colonization
our families brought with us, and found
on this continent when we arrived.

In the morning we'll make breakfast,
begin again with nourishment, fire. Tonight,
from a floating dock, we watch as the sun
falls through the ocean above ocean that makes its way
inland over mountains. A crossroads, you say.
Before we go to sleep, we'll step close-close to
that tree, as tribute touch its bark, its roots.

Tomorrow a whale will show us what it is to be
the depth itself—where the waves from across
meet the shallows. But first, we stand, prepare.
Where three stairs used to lead to something
in the past, at the threshold where the ingrowth
has already taken back the place they led to.

We pour libations and, beside them,
place the smoke. As you make orasyon,
what we first mistake for a feather
is a seed that floats across,
and we won't know whether it reaches
ground, finding what it needs to grow, or if
it catches another current, simply keeps on rising.

II.

Kamatayan Was Exactly Correct

My lola's chewing is marvelously toothless.

Adobo shines her gums,
she cracks the bones for marrow's extra salt.

Trace the letters, she might say, but never does,
the language of salt.

Why would she say anything in a language she can't speak?

The story she salts with the power out
has a candle pointing up its face.

A minute after the fright, and my
breath is still scuffled. This ocean between

my sweat for her, my tears and her village
salt. I took no jeepney through the cordillera

when her chewing left.

I try to put myself to sleep by counting
the cackles she threw at me

after those jokes would leap from her tongue

in one language to land on my ears
as sounds I could almost place. Holding us

even after the bone-clean of a meal,
bowl-tilt and swipe. *Be more mischief!*

She never said that either, though it floats
like doorstep gossip, tilted

in the boast of continuity
wearing her bundok smile. Is Lola also salt?

Asin. One part who I am, one part
where I'm from? A story she only tells me

years after she died? Tonight, Undas,
as if my movements are made from the micro-

physics of her movements: when I brush my hair,
I brush the knots: out of hers. This mess is also

    true. In my hand, our backhand one-arm broom. The line

from my hips to shoulders, fends
toward the curve of hers.

    This awe—

become what binds me to salt,
the part my broom can't sweep away.

A Little Troubled Wundr (Just as Much for You as for Them)

Beside the search tent—four-post canopy hub—after that midnight
apparition caused three of you to trace a path of smoke

back from where the vision left and around
this roundabout, what you do is hold enough

together to get the tweens playing Charades. You must remember
how your niece's cousins wouldn't let her win at Uno

around her hospital bed the fall that told you to try
stay here. Give thanks she survived. So few truly do.

The next night, after the first novena,
penannular: you really only need one to get drunk

on behalf of all of you. In the roundabout you circled thrice
the eve of Eric's body finally getting river-found

(you will never forget the rending of the air from Niki's wail)
you pick up the game of Charades you started with the girls

instead of telling them—not yet but soon—about the encounter's
vividness, the answer it portended, the questions in the smoke.

Begin with the gesture for "movie." Now, that two-handed
capital "T" standing in for "The." Find a way to janky-

dance the middle word. Your face grotesque so the kids
can't help but laugh. Inside yourself you're

doubled over to your knees, tears out at the curb.
Outside, on one good leg, you're jumping up and down.

We Hinge (For What's Left Out)

The most recent dish I burnt was an attempt to add oxtail to day-old sinigang. One of the bones took on the shape of a bird-star at its centre. I freaked out like I deserve a deep-deep punish, and it's haunting me since.

Something else that haunts me: a summer week years ago when I learned lesson after lesson, and every single one was accompanied by bee-sting.

It was during a youth camp at which I was a mentor, on a beautiful stretch of land in another province that still hurts. Picture me catching lessons as they floated by. By the end of the first day: swelling on both calves and arms, forehead above right eyebrow, left pinky knuckle. Pushing a fingernail at those last two in order, here is one that stuck: we cannot change the past, and yet everything we do changes the shapes in our past.

Should I feel sorrier to the youth whose lessons I think I stole, or to the flowers who were calling bees for pollen? This is not a metaphor: I'm the type of person creatures had to die for, just so I tilt out my ears (and cringe for years after) at words like *forgiveness*.

I have tried to invent Forgiveness Mudra several times. Tomorrow, again.

∽

Another being who hurts still: my oldest friend
on this sacred continent—alive in an apartment
where our 1990s teenage brown-boy poses
litter the floor. Their scratches of understanding
our masculinity couldn't handle. His eyes that bloodshot night
when he tried to prove who he wasn't, the meanness in his telling
as if it wasn't love—losing even then the fullness of himself.
Behind our poses, that lifting fog the camera
prefers to any steady threshold. Maybe also
a form of sweeping. Because the photo album, empty,
is a body for what is safe to keep.

∽

I hope you already know what I'm going to say now: bees are holy.
They sacrifice that we might know the scent of faith in spring.
You might already guess I struggle to be better.
There's so many more lessons for me to learn, and only so many bees.

We're ugly when we stretch toward our beautifulest selves. Because of how arduous that stretch. Ugly enough that, futile as it gets, the holiest of creatures might offer us their only sting. Their very life: sacrifice.

∽

To inhabit is to absorb.
Should I believe what I just said?

This is only a little tongue of dirt, a little divination: the city you leave
in me sweeps on bees and elder trees carved by hands. Beat-down alleys, too.

And so much glinting I wear but just can't call my own.

What is mine is the moments that stretched when I struggled against another boy, who couldn't tell me he didn't want me to leave into migration. All that we had shared succumbing to the wildness in his eyes—. We never quite get back the tenderness we lose, and someone else is always punished.

(*You know: like your smile in the photo I took of you that spring, before I left and returned, changed but not enough to find my way to you.*)

∽

Picture a honeybee's after-sting body begin to wobble, to fall
and curl. Its memory in my body, the land it falls onto. The air—
with another momentary fragrance—moves in to fill the space it fell from.

Jalebi, Jolly Bee, guava, rambutan.

My teeth are only perfect where the braces failed to take.

If a thing can pull you, it can hurt you: and that's the prize.

To inhabit, as does ink.

The bird-star at the centre of all I've burnt, an anchor. To be reminded when the punctuation doesn't want to let me go. Smoke, back into wings. The charring taken in by my nostrils as I scrub into the pot a spiral marking at its base that seeps into its future work.

That meat-poor sauce, rich again in lingering.

Mountain Walk Offering for My Godson

May you outgrow many pairs of shorts, Anak.
And if a dryer doesn't get them first,
your socks might inch down past your heels
bothering your arch and toes. That pattern will turn
to wearing thin, to changing style.

Those dryers will continue to take your socks.
If I didn't already know the danger-cost of this,
I would ask you to invent a drying machine
that gives back as many socks as you feed it,
but my dreams aren't yours. Bless that.

Despite our best intentions, if we reach thirst,
the water in us calling for more water,
we should have responded sooner. Cramps do come
to an end. When you work, remember, that's stardust
under your fingernails; stardust, bird poo, everything
between. Yes, this earth. Learn to make your fingertips

the aroma of garlic. Your parents have scars,
please be gentler than me when you touch their ridges,
some are older than them, older than Lola's lola: all of them
an attempt at healing. You and your sister—dalawalang
sayo—may you always share facing each other and fight

back to back. Islands born from one volcano, clay
forged in fire, spirits given breath. The two of you
will teach me—pens to scraps of paper, laughing
in your indoor socks, making up ancient
symbols as if from actual memory: audacity, divinity—
there are things we learn somehow not to lose.

Wundrkut Forever Ghazal

A turntable skratched-up cento

Where are you now? Do we gotta say farewell tonight? *So many of us wonder.*
God sobs in my arms, a wounded gazelle tonight. *They stay for wonder.*

Up in a pot of rice, up from a human zoo. Twisting, sleeping heads of monsters.
Rupture the root. Route: all the places we came *to*, we came *from wonder.*

Nights he rocked shows, the itch of this tune in his hands. Temples *of boom*,
pyramid of afternoons, carving with his hands. The sweat *he gave for wonder.*

Derecho, emergency. A snap built up in the sound on every panicked highway.
Yesterday, candy: salt-water taffy, tsokolate—*the taste of wonder.*

Reading: setlist crumpled in back pocket. Winding waists, can't forget the glow.
Ellipsis: folding the harmonies holding you, *Niki forgave your wonder.*

Knowing what the frame around the portrait knows. The medicine hurts,
too. Its honey-smoke in the fog that night, *the smiling face of wonder.*

Unmarked crown & royal. behind a counter. mixer. after. school. skipping
pantry in your chest. Your skratches, consonant. *Mistakes? Raw wonder.*

To be shaped I want, yes, color in my gods. Inventing home
from no words at all. & every empty that carries the stain *of wonder.*

Forward, elbow! Kiss hands to vinyl. Be no one. Be music surgeon, ghost.
Be champion. Let none steal, tear down, or gamble away *your wonder.*

On blood. What feeds—let us steady. Household birds & cats. Such intimacy,
jungle. *Kaps.* A burning leaf perfumes these needs, *its after-ache of wonder.*

Red & blinking, decades you crossfade. In the museum of memory, the missing
songs—chosen, then lost—pursue: *Yo, yo deejay! Accumulate our wonder!*

Engines grinding, rotating, smokin'. Gotta bring some glide around.
Inhaling bassline, *ooh wee*, clinging. Brown. *Its every shade of wonder.*

Visit to where the name is known toward the earth, & heaven
bows down in love without end, the dust there *made of wonder.*

Exist, what if I do? In a few flashes in my beloveds' eyes. Longing & restless,
I know the jugglery of the world's hubbub—*its constant splay of wonder.*

Rifted, Hari, precipice in solar plexus? Can't go on alone? Reach out: be held.
—It's an amulet. I think of Silver, put on Kaya's playlist. *& I pray for wonder*

(Rest. Chew on the thread of silence. Dip in inkwater *before you slip it thru
the needle's only eye. Team Danger.* Life, kiss *forever. Eric's way: of Wundr).*

Poem to Burn: **Prayer to the Living**

Palestinian children use the electricity cables as a swing in Gaza
—Video by Ahmad Ibrahim, Posted by Susan Muaddi Darraj,
April 20, 2024

If my niece throws her limbs in every direction trying not to fall
then falls and scrapes her knee, she might or might not
reach for a hand to pull her up. Legs back above the wheels
spinning at her feet. Next time I call, I'll ask her if she still
names it when she falls down. There was a visit before that
when, as I crouched close enough to catch her but not so close
that she might let go a climbing hand to keep mine out of her way,
she clambered up from the floor and into her high chair over and over
for an hour. Telling herself herself by name, "get up," she'd climb, barely
pause, tell herself, "get down," climb down. Hands over feet, tiny,
slightly faster most each time. Finally she said, "got it," nodded, stayed
in her high chair. Having placed into her body a muscle memory
nobody could give her. This might be how the word *sigarilyo*
is shortened and deepened from much repetition into just *yosi*—
its ending and beginning. In the process of turning the word around,
you must fall through a portal in your own centre at the moment
when you extricate the middle of the word, so that the meaning
for *smoker* might become, "one who offers smoke." The word
smoke itself transforms, through this falling, also. Into: "the longing
in a fire for those places the flame can't reach." Across ocean
soon as soon, another child might fall to the ground and hear
her name and laugh. May there be no bombing around her. Let no hands
need to be proffered unless she reaches out. In her own unrubbled town,
where the wires have been given back electricity. And she and her friends
haven't quite internalized the steps for how to convert them into swings.

A Pavement Sweeper's Quarry

This street is a moneylender's duty crowned in smoke. And skin remembers to cherish its own noise. The creaking earth might be a thing to hear.

Avoid the knees of things, I say: they kick.

ஒ

Here, on the morning ride to work, I'm jealous at the trolley doors: they get to yawn. I would say the city is only mouth if it didn't hear: we want to stay.

And here, we bury the summer of ourselves—in traffic jam. A single glance at rearview, and headlights gawk for hours, a headlight stream.

We do not want to hover like a line of fog, a river's shadow, but slower: shadows in conversation, gentle only when we don't bother expecting to be heard.

ஒ

Let me tell you of the gentleness my aspirations keep me from. I want to reminisce how my sister called the dryer "fighting fighting," but it always ends with the labour of folding. We're all of us mules for history, loading it on our backs. History, that merchant of itself. That clothing dryer.

ஒ

Stay. Marrow me. Marrow what I am, skin too. The bones of my speech hide me from the meat my teeth have stripped. Whatever is hungry to be eaten, offer a perfect dustpan's life.

Meanwhile, our daily waste: stipend to a rat. Succulent, evergreen, deciduous, grass: we harvest. To earth, we give the dignity of the stepped-upon. We want to stay. To airsong, we give flinch—

River Pier Offering for Sistar and Lolo

the body is not a thing to escape.
—Cynthia Dewi Oka, "Post-Election Song of Myself"

My sister in navigation, from another migration, lights up
a childhood story, passes me a drag. That's when Lolo's ghost appears
to take one also. In her story, which is both butterfly and knife—
while Lolo smokes and nods his head along—she's telling me that body means,
must always mean: *worth grieving*. Even though she knows she can't
just turn around anywhere and feel that in the human breaths
exhaling in her direction. It's enough to make you smoke.
Luckily we're on the river edge of town, and the only people
we've seen today: coyotes lumbering across the road with open mouths.
A wildness recalling who we've been to this city since we started our ongoing
arrival: because even when we were, we couldn't be its dogs. I wish I
could've witnessed Lolo's galavanting days, as we galavant kind of
like coyotes in city. My sis writes so beautiful that, if she read me a poem right then,
I would have almost thrown her off this pier into the river. A tugboat
pulls a log boom many times its size. Its wake. The shore. The ripples.
Her story, it keeps me from biting my tongue (nothing gets passed down
through generations like silence). Now I'm asking if she can hear
whatever Lolo sung to keep his feet moving as he Death-Marched
from Bataan in April's warming rain, a song that took his voice
a generation to return in the form of lullaby. Maybe he hid it
in the smoke. I say *ambush* and mean his escape from one,
but my sis knows ambush all too well. What it is to scour
a rock—or turning rooster vane—for signs of coming blood,
I wish both of them didn't have to know. Here, where our usefulness
became the question we asked ourselves instead of love,
we leave each other tunnels in our stories. So, even if one of us
doesn't make it out, the other one might find us.
It's my bitter trash-talk face she cackle-snaps, old man style with yosi
dangling out my mouth and squint, chastising some imaginary chump
for doing shit I might have used to do. Me, I'm truly

truly lucky, to meet a chosen sibling who can tell a story like my lolo
never got to tell me. I wish that both of them had only suffered griefs
like my privilege afforded me: how I've gotten—together with beloveds
and in song—to hold the devastation of a single lost
beloved, slow. When Sistar sings, I hear the lullaby's rev
the Death March failed to take from Lolo
Mauro. His body walking on any day but that
and walking on that day, too. I see it now. Sistar: he loves her. Beyond
the body of her words, a hunger that turns a fork into a hand. Like Lolo's
hand at my childhood mouth: holding my mouth quiet, no. Teaching it
to open. Between us, the smoke improvises its own lineage.

As if Drawn

from gazing directly at the sun, the faintest
mocking, quarter notes of silence
who graze from roof-flat to cedar bough and mock
the quarter notes between the mockingbirds'

falling now, worried as a lullaby
at the edge of sleep. Sleep says nothing,
lifts the needle back onto the record
after Curtis Mayfield's final kindness.

That rising melt of sound
wants to lick the couch in the other room,
its crackle unscratched. Perhaps
to hear the layers of gaps
beneath his falsetto body,
your smoke is green, it's all in words.

What surfaces?
Dot by dot, an image through another
needle, piercing into skin.

Dear inner voice of doubt, right
now you're equal portions rot
eaten by grass and household fly. Perfectly,
and in all fault I mean just that,
receive this boiled advice as I have yours:
against what you demand of me, there
is none, no joy you don't deserve.

Braided Ghazal [Rest]

Co-written with Faisal Mohyuddin

Because a temple is only shelter, a body hungry to house another god,
we yearn for pilfered offerings, for more than a feeble breath of rest.

Am I wrong to say that every small offering is also a kind of theft?
Or is it loss? Because wounds live within wonder, neither is a form of rest.

As children we didn't know the ways we wounded the mountains, still
cannot safely read beyond each other's skin. Our Himalayas cannot yet rest.

A mountain is a temple raised up by the earth—its clouds, oceans mocking
the low-lying land, saying, *You've climbed only so far, afraid to face the rest.*

When I say worship, you call me a beast. I trumpet breath. It knows
every prayer is a plea to forge more space for acceptance—for a purer rest.

Night is touched by the torch of a coming day, a revelation asking
if monsters in us are just a growling need, or a suffering wishing for rest.

To enter any room is to become an offering—perhaps there's no such rest
on earth as an empty room. A song crosses an ocean, seeks a place to rest.

Because a body's sanctuary ends too soon, listening must be our temple,
abundant with the shadow of *I'm sorry—in peace, Mere Bhai, chal. Rest.*

III.

Windowsill Offering for Eric

In the crematorium's service room, taking clumsy, ginger turns around the cardboard holding your body, such a thin distance, 4 generations of multi-iteration family scrawl and draw our messages for you to take. An act of reaching. Even here, the squeal and fight of children over markers carries what's most sombre.

This act of releasing you to mark how we must begin to hold you another way, a promise in touch, which no one can live up to constant: from outside the chapel's doors, through the service room, around and down the hall—Sade's "By Your Side" playing off your celebrant's phone as we arrange ourselves—one hand reaching forward to the next shoulder, in to the shoulders of your closest and your closest blood, finally onto Niki's.

Hers, the most difficult task. Even as it's her finger on the switch: when she presses it to give your body to fire—held and utterly alone—none of us are free of it. Our hope, which is also our fear: that we reach across to the other side with you, that the messages we wrote carry us with them in the flame.

Ingat

March 2020

Taking off my outside clothes
in the doorway, a kind of prayer. I strip

and it's my asking for the safety of those
I live with. I had to go out. Yes—

when it was groceries and soap. Yes, too,
for addiction. I still smoke. I got the message
when my boy in England enumerated for us

how and why we need to get ready. Also to stop sending
the memes giving us levity with our solitude. Sorry, brother. I share

what's funny anyway. Our desperation belongs
everywhere right now. Doors or no, someone is entering

a space they share with people they love
or tolerate. Or like or just help out or want to touch or wish they could get
away from. The door, barely closed and I'm

praying in my socks. May I not have brought
what we're afraid of catching

the way I bring how thin
my threads already are. Shouting

before I left the apartment carries
an older poison. I act like I can leave it
on the shut side of a door.

Windowsill Offering for Niki

Do you also have a habit of feeling the curtain's
crease from across the room? Reaching,
feeling in your fingers what is out of reach?
To read the scuff marks on the wall
as constellations, etched by names we lost,
as if the space where a person was is a person, too?
And everything we are becomes an interruption.

∽

One day may we learn to poke circles into the air
in front of an altar with an incense stick—let the smoke
guide us in a dance with our dead.

To Hum Its Dizziness Like Sugar in Tea

A photo carries its own skeleton along death's emulsifying road.

Because every box and border dreaming of a sash, thin enough to render
scissors obsolete.

If any divine pauses: the first remittance.

Or rest, or shelter.

I will always thank the day I turned towards these mountains here and saw
not the country I feared wants me dead or gone or totally subsumed, but
mountains, volcanic. Cousins
to those who made the islands my nanay is from, and beautiful even if they weren't.

The deities I brought with me and seek, may they never become a pipeline dug into this land.

A passport and failure's addiction, amen.
I hold, I thumb its pages,

splinter that promise and accept the twinkled fumbling of our own pockets for signs
of ourselves, of the watered earth, the earth who asks for a goddess of what's lost.

Sometimes the most beauty someone like me can offer is to not belong.

Leafing through the photos I developed, I pretend to show them
to Anagolay. Pour some tea, a little on the parching road.

This is for the hands who hold back any machine's encroachment onto land's own thirst.
For hands redoing another's braid or pulling baggage off a belt, hands reaching for lovers
across oceans or enclosures. Aged brown hands—so sweet—holding each other in this place
less for love than just to keep their balance.

Sometimes what we hold is a chant, a single chant for what we fear
is in danger of reaching the deity of what's lost,
a chant for remembrance which carries *work* which carries *attend* which carries
the *take*, the *care* needed for what *come back* must carry.

This chant can never belong to me if it only belongs to mine.

Chris says that a photograph is not taken, but made. What parts of us
learn to construct what our naked eye can't see? Maybe this as well:

if my feet are balancing on the lament of a railroad track or playing footsie naked,
whether my hands are dirt-bound by my labour or echoes
on another's skin missing her actual love, maybe not the eye that's open but the other,
holding like a dragonfly's buzz to the part of the world that's dreaming.

Anting-Anting: May You Lose Your Balance

while undressing for a lover beside the kitchen freezer.
The clatter, the broom that falls: you will of course sweep up

that dessert you pushed aside. For now,
cling to each other like tattoos cling

from beneath the skin. Around you both, that freezer's
hum, holy as your foreignness.

I wish you the wafting of spice across a busy street, head nods
as you jaywalk. A fried flour convo hollowed of beginnings,

hollowed of decrees. Of the arches in your shovel,
may the wind ask only the song of what you choose to plant.

Mid-Bridge Offering to Bataan for Lolo's Second Sight / *Bataan Death March Responds with a Joke from Lolo's Hospital Room*

He survived you for my nanay to even exist, and—

word to his anting-anting—an ambush he predicted, too. The ambush

was by his countrymen fighting for their freedom

against his army's support of an American military base.

The way I don't tell that part is the way I never talk about

arguing not to do my chores minutes after Tupac's "Dear Mama"

had me bawling into supplication at my nanay's feet. Okay, I didn't quite

do supplication then, but I definitely got my crying face

all over her good sleeves. You see, all of my second sight

is second-hand. Maybe, like my lolo's platoon, I just learned

to be nearby when someone else is seeing. My lolo's spirit sight,

before it saved his platoon's lives, is why he quit playing cards for money.

He didn't want to be called a cheat, as if it was his fault the cards

chose him to show their highest faces. That was always the superpower

I wanted to inherit, not the life of an orphan selling candles

in a miracle church to feed his younger siblings. Not the kind of life

where you need second sight just to see your kids and love again.

This is my favourite story of your lolo, who lived another
50 years after surviving me, the jeepney rise, another war
(you would say he was on the wrong side of), that ambush you know
he predicted, tire fires on the land he bought and—illiterate—learned
he had signed away, a scoundrel's reputation nipping at the heels
of his lifelong love, frog-leg meals dug from paddy rice, children's needs,
grandkids from where I'll stay to where your sister climbs. Only to stub his toe and have
its infection take his leg, his laugh a while, and finally his life
amputation by amputation. After flying back to my arkipelago,
just to be there after his next surgery, his daughter
arrives at hospital. The front desk, unattended. The halls behind it,
empty, too. Itched up by mosquitos from before, "Maybe it's their lunch,"
she says, instead of, "Please, not yet" (the thanks she gave
for making it on the flight starting to dissipate), listening
down each hallway, finally catching her ear on some overlapping
laughter. Its echoes. She follows them right up to his door.
Opens it. His convalescent bed, surrounded by every nurse
on this ward it seems, them crowded toward him, shoulders
shaking up and down—you know you love this part—slow to make space
for the old man's daughter to get through, slow to quiet fully
back to the seriousness she brings—gladly, loudly, in your mother's way.

Letter to the Deity Who Told Me Arriving Here Is Difficult as Welcome

Dear Kabunian,

I was pulling card after card. Searching for you, days, years, seeking
your story. Clay, water, breath, spirit. All of it can't be loss. My searching interrupted
by a bird's headlong flap into the glass. That single sound. Then, the small-wing

flutter trapped between the insect screen and the sliding door.
My urge to take a photo first. Its plight, so beautiful. The voice inside
demanding I instead wrench that screen clean off the roller. That flying might

continue in that bird. If I call the half-dull drum beat of my wings
a freedom song, it's all imagination. Some feathers must be left behind,
and I love you not just with the self I want to be, but with my demons, too.

The way you gave your buhay to our bodies, shaped us
from the soup of earth itself, and faced us generous
with the ugly in ourselves, me facing that bird I wanted to capture

more than set it free. The yellow warbler that hit the window
on the other side, I had already released it back to ground like my lolo's name.
But this one, downy woodpecker I think, reminds me in its leaving

that exile living also includes joy. Are you like that? Fascinated
by our feathers being roughed by the places that won't let our wingspan
reach its full? I feel my own voice as a sweetness-ache you wish

for me to fight for and release. For so long I wished the healer Babaylan
weren't fed to crocodiles (those beings whose mouth is always saying
Welcome). And also in that bird: the songs their survivors learned

from the crocodile, its killing welcomed into a carrying of song.
Chasm become bridge—the faith a bangka holds that another shore exists,
and can be reached. I turn back to the lake, row this kayak out to its centre,

pause. The sun-cut waves at push and tilt, spiral the vessel. Let them. There: that tree whose branches reveal a kind of face, and on the other side: as if from out horizon, another larger sudden bird on flap-approaching wing.

Yes, Crosshatch—off the Docks— an Offering for You as Well

City we came to, you whisper
whispery enough the fires we brought might nuzzle
closer in to hear. Your footstep. Your shipping

container serenade. An uncertain mythology
whose living contents are each a sacrifice
imagining how to reach. How to pivot

between two gods faded as the velocities
from quenching stars. Their nightly arrival,
with or without light. City, you lean into the mountains

like the boys my boys and I were
leaning against a wall we cannot own. The wind mouths
whatever sentence is next in a horizon. This wooden dock,

a skipping stone's distance to the thing that reaches
every other side. And here, a busted cinderblock admonishes
with its turtle face: pour salt from your meridian and turn

this corner, you will find in the square
pieces of sea an infinity of precipices. I ask
how much of who I am is in those boxes

we never unpacked after migration. Here
is the arm with which I used to scrub
a charter boat's bannister free of Brasso

over, again, filling my pages with no promise
but labour. In every fingerprint I refuse to leave behind
on any brass another must re-shine, the grip

I fail to reach with, the whisper in
my hands. Like breath at the ridges of a corrugated
mirror offering no reflection. I pour

my drink to the sacrifice of wells. Your gift, City,
is in you. As in all those who sunlight yearns
to touch—like any ripening or sudden-flaunted lung.

Poem to Burn: **Attend**

A border will only persist as bench to rest at
on a stroll—call it respite, serve tasty refreshments.
At every station, cup to cup, a pouring
back-and-forth: those whose names traverse
in the form of libations: welcome.
Bereft of any detention centre,
bereft of separation. Rivers
walk, back towards
faith in
us

Train Station Offering for Popsi

When the coming of another grave
jabs at me like harvest, stolen. And the flame
inside consumes. I'm reminded of
the losses I still fear, which you've
already faced. And yours, my father,
I will kick it away like a rooster,
talon tied to blade—but not the care
we are both finally learning we must hold
tight as any blade we've learned to wield.
Like ash, like loss to the Goddess of Lost Things.

When a body ascends away from reason,
I wish it was enough to speak
one missing name as you have mine, a call
when memory left you. Instead of pointing my attentions
out, this digging I need in storm: this glory of tears,
I bind my pain, my labour to something closer.

On those days I pocket dialed my homie,
kapwatid long since drowned. For those moments
when feathers of my hope and yours
are a bother stuck at lips. I don't wish on you
this desolation whose texture is of silt, velour
against the nerves. No more days when the work
leaves you unable to thank
your sweat: down to a toenail,
your presence is worth my awe
for newfound constellations, opening
the narrow sky above a single wall.

Coffee, toothbite, styrofoam. Styrofoam and cargo.
Outside the train stop, a hawk: how it glances upside
then side to side between each pulling
redsplash bite of fallen pigeon. Have you also stared
into the crankled dark absorbed by windows—
praying a deity of lost things might visit—
bloomed your fingers at their ghosts?

Then you might feel dizzy. Here, a spell:
whether giant lavender or dwarf wisteria,
whether cedar or banyan tree, fruit-
bearing or root, concrete or quarried
rain shadow valley: say body, say love.

May you feel easy
in your skin. May the language of ancestors
tattoo the ground you walk on,
back from all the places where their failings
gather as a congregation of mercies.

That time in the mall, the hand of your friend
we asked you to drop because you're both men, I wish
for you to take it up again, for me to walk beside you unafraid
of the belonging that ranks. Sure, I've had to
practice losing my gentleness
since the first young wound. But there are days
for the blade of full refusal, days for a simple whisper.

What is thick: the cold, the doses of exclusion, the generous
human contribution to earthly hurt, the song
that pulls me from the knot of my mouth
back toward searching the low round hills
in all of your seven souls. My monster is a bargain,
despair dropped easy like bushmeat in
the boiling pot. It simmers
like memories of your dwindling siblings,
multiplies my shadows, dipped
how dreams dip into the mountains.

Counting the insults alive
in your ear, the collapses,
the collapses, counting them now
I hear your voice the day we almost
lost you, "It's a small life," you said
and I wanted to shout that yours,
which brought me here, No, it couldn't
be! But you sang out my name,
I called the ambulance, and I've been
shying away from telling you this since.

Today, I try to grow small. Enough to hear
your body—into the groove—
expand. The stars, the city lights
who swallow them: they do not leave you,
but gleam. Like oil spill and candle
glut—like a forest burning.

∽

What is sharp and thin in me,
I carry. Like you carry: the languages
you couldn't give me: the strength
you still save: the mischief I ask that you will
wear again when you return: to this place
where all that has seen famine
returns. If each day is orphan
and river to a goddess of lost things,
as my lament also dies down to whisper
curved, hemmed like a dawn who knows
death is the only tongue
freed of incantations; and light
flows from the ladle you still offer:
as a seed's journey to harvest, reaching—I drink.

Windowsill Offering to the Lingling-O

I ask the cards—

call back a loved one, one whose body can no longer be found.
A card out the deck leaps on my first shuffle, and homegirl
stokes a vision: now arkipelago, now this crescent cove.
Isang bagsak!—a sound to begin.

And here, the echoes—

an ocean's time away. My homegirl senses, as a blur, then fully sees our guide.
Floating in front of her and above the shallows, their starcloth
dipping ripples to begin. Rippling again to stand inside the room.

Tears followed by laughter—

they cradle a residence for spirits. *To begin*, she begins,
I saw what seeks you.

Listen in ritual—

to begin. Rhythm, to begin. She waves a hand at what will shift. Lid to begin, of clay
Adug; incisions to begin; necklace to begin; tree bark faces, rain-touched to begin.

To begin—

an ocean's reach of time away, the amulet and scar your mother gave:
calling back to a part of you already accepting all of you, Bahala na
you reach, a part of you you didn't know you do not need to seek.

NOTES TO THE POEMS

The Cigarette Is Pretext: Smoke Rises from Within: For Lola Mercedez / After Amelia Bane / After Jon Sands / After Nazim Hikmet, Li-Young Lee, and Claudia Rankine, with title interpolated from Yannis Ritsos, tr. Karen Emmerich & Edmund Keeley

Zoom Call with Lunar Moth on the Wall, and Tilting: After Seema Reza / After Maureen Seaton

Feel at How It's Etched: After Willie Perdomo / After Harrison Pratt

Windowsill Offering to Anagolay, Goddess of Lost Things : After Barbara Jane Reyes / After Keenan Norris / After a conversation with Selina Boan & Brandi Bird

Poem to Burn: From Spiral and Storm: After Kimi King

Windowsill Offering for My Nanay, with Help from Analogay: For Fe Malagayo Alluri

When I Walk in She's Mixing Someone's Drink, Hitting the Notes on "How Will I Know," and Later We Together-Laugh at an Inside Joke on Us: After Whitney Houston (1985) / After Lisa Lisa & Cult Jam's "Lost in Emotion" (1987)

Threshold Offering for Crossroads That Keep on Forming: For David; the epigraph is from David Maduli's "Microclimates," which first appeared in *Cream City Review*, Vol. 45, No. 2 (2021)

Origin Story: After Harilaos Stefanakis

Kamatayan Was Exactly Correct: After Amina Saïd / After Ilya Kaminsky / After Jennifer Maramba, Jana Lynne Umipig & Verma Soraya Zapanta, with title reference to "Kamatayan – The Sulod Trio" (Jana Lynne Umipig, *Kapwa Tarot*)

A Little Troubled Wundr (Just as Much for You as for Them): After Niki Cardeno, Mahal, & Apo Adman / After Ria & Mya and Tala & Kaya

We Hinge (For What's Left Out): For and after Muriel Leung, cf. Marcella Kroll ("Relief," *Sacred Symbols Oracle Deck)*

Mountain Walk Offering for My Godson: Word to both Apollo and Zuleikha

Wundrkut Forever Ghazal: A turntable skratched-up cento for and after DJ Wundrkut Eric Cardeno. Most of this poem's text is gathered, gratefully, from the 16 ghazals and 3 songs below, following the rules that—apart from the final pair of couplets—more than half of each couplet must be sampled, with the first word of each couplet drawn from one of the sources (with allowance for samples, skratches, and interpolations that play with tense, pluralization, sense, and word order):

"Tonight" by Agha Shahid Ali, "Ghazal for Dogeaters" by Danni Quintos, "Portrait of the artist as Manananggal" by Maria Bolaños, "Hustle" by John Murillo, "Derecho Ghazal" by Luisa A. Igloria, "Red Ghazal" by Aimee Nezhukumatathil, "Holding You" by Purple Hearts Social Club (both original and live versions), "Ghazal for Becoming Your Own Country" by Angel Nafis, "Ghazal for White Hen Pantry" by Jamila Woods, "Ghazal" by Edil Hassan, "Ghazal" by Gunnar Ekelöf (tr. Rika Lesser), "Infinity Ghazal Beginning with Lice and Never Ending with Lies" by Tarfia Faizullah, "Ghazal: With Prayer" by Zeina Hashem Beck, "Hip-Hop Ghazal" by Patricia Smith, "From the Ghazals of Ghalib" (XL) by Ghalib (tr. Aijaz Ahmad & WS Merwin), "Ghazal" by Jigar Morabadi, "Inkwater" by DJ Wundrkut, and "Kiss of Life" by Sade

Poem to Burn: Prayer to the Living: After Ahmad Ibrahim via Susan Muaddi Darraj / After Luisa A. Igloria via David Maduli; originally for the children of Gaza in general—and still for them always—this poem is now dedicated especially to Tala Abu Ajwa, with love to Zuleikha and to our Tala Boo

A Pavement Sweeper's Quarry: For Neelanjana Banerjee

River Pier Offering for Sistar and Lolo: For Cynthia / For Mauro Malagayo; the epigraph is from Cynthia Dewi Oka's "Post-Election Song of Myself," which appeared in the now-defunct *Blueshift Journal*, and was the title of a much shorter poem which appeared in the next issue of the same journal

As if Drawn: For generations of Curtis Mayfield's music, with special thanks to "I Believe in You" (duet with Sandra St. Victor, 1996)

Braided Ghazal [Rest]: Co-written with Faisal Mohyuddin

Windowsill Offering for Eric: After Godwyn Young / After Sol Diana & Carlo Sayo

Windowsill Offering for Niki: After Daisy Thompson, Rianne Svelnis & Emmalena Fredriksson / After Holly Kang

To Hum Its Dizziness Like Sugar in Tea: After Julius Lester / After Mahmoud Darwish / After Arthur Kayzakian and Eunice Andrada, with an interpolation of Fe Malagayo Alluri

Anting Anting: May You Lose Your Balance: For Tanzila Ahmed, with an interpolation of Patrick Rosal

Mid-Bridge Offering to Bataan for Lolo's Second Sight / *Bataan Death March Responds with a Joke from Lolo's Hospital Room*: For Lolo Mauro and Fe Malagayo Alluri / After Anand Bakshi, with an interpolation of "Siyam ng Rattan" (Jane Lynne Umipig, *Kapwa Tarot*)

Letter to the Deity Who Told Me Arriving Here Is Difficult as Welcome: For and After Apo Adman / After Ruby Singh

Yes, Crosshatch—off the Docks—an Offering for You as Well: After KPU WSS, with thanks to Jen Currin / After China Miéville / After Amanda Fuller

Poem to Burn: Attend: Invited by Kenji Liu / Written in *X* form, with a shoutout to David Maduli

Train Station Offering for Popsi: For Krishna Alluri / After Kwame Dawes and Marcella Kroll

Windowsill Offering to the Lingling-O: After Niki Silva / After Chris Abani / After Phanuel Antwi, Shaunga Tagore, and Julay, with interpolations of Jana Lynne Umipig

ACKNOWLEDGEMENTS

Gratefulness to the editors, special folio editors, staff, organizers, and volunteers of the following venues, through which versions of these poems first appeared, sometimes under different titles:

Adi Magazine	"Letter to the Deity Who Told Me Arriving Here Is Difficult as Welcome"
Apogee	"Kamatayan Was Exactly Correct" (also published in *poetry in canada*)
Blog This Rock	"Ingat"
Contemporary Verse 2	"Windowsill Offering to Anagolay, Goddess of Lost Things" "Windowsill Offering for My Nanay, with Help from Anagolay" "A Little Troubled Wundr (Just as Much for You as for Them)"
Cutbank	"Windowsill Offering to the Lingling-O"
The Margins	"A Pavement Sweeper's Quarry" (also published in *poetry in canada*)
Magdaragat	"River Pier Offering for Sistar and Lolo"
Massachusetts Review	"Origin Story"
Michigan Quarterly Review	"Feel at How It's Etched"
Ovenbird	"When I Walk in She's Mixing Someone's Drink, Hitting the Notes on 'How Will I Know,' and Later We Together-Laugh at an Inside Joke on Us"

Poem-a-Day	"Poem to Burn: From Spiral and Storm"
Poetry	"Train Station Offering for Popsi" "Wundrkut Forever Ghazal"
Puerto del Sol	"To Hum Its Dizziness Like Sugar in Tea"
Sepia Journal	"We Hinge (For What's Left Out)"
Şerābi Zine	"Braided Ghazal [Rest]"
Split This Rock	"The Cigarette Is Pretext: Smoke Rises from Within" (*Best of the Net* 2022; also published in *poetry in canada*)
Tinderbox	"Zoom Call with Lunar Moth and the Wall, and Tilting"
Unmargin.org	"Poem to Burn: Attend" (also published in *Capitalism Nature Socialism*)
Wildness	"Yes, Crosshatch—Off the Docks—an Offering for You as Well"
18 Million Rising	"Anting-Anting: May You Lose Your Balance"

GRATITUDES ON THE WINDOWSILL

From the root of me, I'm grateful. As Jason said: "to you, yes you, to all of you who have lifted me..." It's time to surrender this work to the world. I'm scared. Give thanks. May it awaken to the hearts of all those who need it most. You are connected now to all those who transformed the poems and myself in relation to them: a cacophonic harmony of salamats, shukriyas & thanks. You who are in this work, thank you for witnessing me: I trust that you feel it. To any who know your names should be here yet don't find them below: I'm sorry, down to the purest earth of me. Like Lola, Ammamma, Lolo & Tata, the spiritual truth is that you're here.

The origin family who holds me through all. Momsi, Popsi, Rina (be that) and all those who hold you. There will never be enough offerings. Mahal, our ongoing reunion: moonrise, rainbow, water bird, Lalahon. And on. Tala, I will keep on trying to respond to your questions, and I can't wait for us to collaborate on our project(s). About grief, yes, and also about joy! From the lands I carry within to the keepers of those—Ts'uubaa-asatx land, Cowichan Tribes land, Musqueam, Squamish, and Tsleil-Waututh lands—that hold me now. My guides, on every side from every element, every day. Word to Apo Adman. All the learners and emerging writers from classrooms to zoom rooms to community centres (may your visions come through, may the writing you are here to bring cross the bridge you build into this world) and mentors (you also) from before and during: thank you for teaching me. And, even if you don't remember: SJS, who told me years ago a thing I'm still trying to learn—"sometimes the medicine chooses you."

Extended family, blood and chosen, for many years of such deep support. Amanda Fuller, Cecily Nicholson, sistar Cynthia Dewi Oka, Cyrille Spale, paré David Maduli, Garrett Bryant, brother Jas Gill, pinsan Jen Maramba, Junie Désil, Kimi King, Maria Bolaños, Mercedes Eng, Naomi

Horii, Neela Banerjee, Niki Silva, Paul Oka, Phanuel Antwi, Sara Kendall, Seema Reza, Sozan Savehilaghi. Word to Amanda, Bill, carla joy & Chris, Dani, Darius & Reid, David, Don, Harri, Jeff, Jon, JR, Laura June, Maria, Maritez, Preeti, Ren, Reza, Robin, Raul, Rup, Sheila, Tita Dori & Tito Godi, Vanessa, and on. Arkipelago & Subcontinent, family I've reconnected to, met for the first time, and am always connected with. In this world and after you left: you're here. Extended-extended fam across this planet, multiple generations, Pangasinan to Palestine to South Van, past the herd of elk grazing down the road.

Some of this work was drafted in, worked out, or revised in communities—online and in person. Word to the makers of these communities, facilitators, co-writers and readers, co-panelists, folks who got down, folks whose labour is always in the moments of expression: Aphotic Theatre, BIPOC Writing Party, Burnaby Art Gallery (Dream Marrow), Cinder Block, Community Building Art Works, The Digital Sala, The Essentials (The Cultch & Soft Cedar), A Gatheration, Geopoetics, The Grind, the How to Be project (EDAM Dance Choreographic Series), Hilot Academy of Binabaylan, Indian Summer Festival, Joy Kogawa House, League of Canadian Poets, Liars of Orpheus (Death Rides a Unicorn), Massy Books & Massy Arts crews, Mental Health, Next Page Press, Sampaguita Press, Surrey Muse, Team Danger, 3-1-1, Vancouver Poetry House, Voices of Color Crew, The World We Want. Grateful acknowledgment to the BC Arts Council and the Canada Council for the Arts, whose support made specific parts of this work possible, and to *The Capilano Review* Writer-in-Residence program and City of Burnaby's Deer Lake Residencies for the time and space to work on several of these poems.

Land, water, strands, hands, and: inspiration + invitation = collaboration. Conversations also, specific to this work and its foundations: Adrian De Leon, Angela Peñaredondo, Anjoli Roy, Anne Bourne, Ashaki Jackson, Ashok Mathur, Baho at the concert, Barbara Jane Reyes, Beverly Walker,

Brandon Wint, Bronwen Tate, Catherine Hernandez, Chiwan Choi, Chris Santiago, Clint Burnham, Cornel Bogle, Cyrus Tasalloti Kashani, Danielle LaFrance, Danny Ramadan, Denise Ferreira da Silva, DJ Su-Comandante Raul Espinoza, D.M. Bradford, Drew Clarke, Edzi'u, Eileen R. Tabios, Elee Kraljii Gardiner, Emily Dundas Oke, Erik Haensel, Erika Chinami Parker, Fay Nass, Fiona Tinwei Lam, Gabrielle Martin, Gordon Grdina via Ruby Singh (the whole Last Prayer Bead!), Hazel Kang, Ina Cariño, Jana Lynne Umipig, Jake Eduardo Vermaas, Jen Currin, Jillian Christmas, Jills Laxamana, Joanne Leow, Karen An-hwei Lee, Kazim Ali, Kemi Craig, Khari Wendell McClelland (those visits with Honey Rose & Poet, I miss most), Khingz, Laura Jew, Laura Van Prooyen, Lydia Kwa, Mai Der Vang, Marc Perez, Maria Maloney, Mendel Skulsk, Michael Mercurio, Michael Nardone, Molly Cross-Blanchard, Muriel Leung, Nathan Adler, Neil Aitken, Nicola Harwood, No'u Revilla, Patricia Massy, Patrick de Belen (that whole gathered room!), Patrick Rosal (*Atang*!), Raji Aujla, Rajiv Mohabir, RC Weslowski, Renée Sarojini Saklikar, Rina Alluri, Rina Garcia Chua, Rolando Gomez Comon, Romila Barryman, Ron Villanueva, Rosa De Anda, Ruby Singh, Ruby Smith Díaz, Sam Roxas-Chua, Sarahlynn Pablo, Sean McGarragle, Setareh Mohammadi, Sham-e-Ali Nayeem, Shaunga Tagore, Sherwin Bitsui, Shireen Soofi, SJ Valiquette, Steffi Tad-y, Stephen Collis, Sunyoung Lee, Trinidad Escobar, Truong Tranh, Valentina Desideri, Vanessa Richards. Amanda Galvan Huynh & Luisa A. Igloria; Carlo Sayo & Sol Diana, Coco Zhou & Diane Hau Yu Wong; Daisy Thompson, Rianne Svelnis & Emmalena Fredriksson; Dani Alcalde-Sidloski, Nathalie De Los Santos & Maria Bolaños; Dina Del Bucchia, Miko Hoffman & Toke Adejoye; Emily Hunter & Namosh Reddy; Erin Robinsong & Michael Datura; Eugene Kung & Ale Lopez; Harsha Walia & Harjap Grewal; Jacquelyn Zong-Li Ross & Deanna Fong; Gabriel Teodros & Ijeoma Oluo; Jessica Poon & Wolfy; Karla Brundage & Allison Paynter; Kawika Guillermo & Alyssa Sy de Jesus; Lauren Lavery & Matea Kulić; MB & Pat; Michal Kozlowski & Shyla Seller; Verma Zapanta & Harvey Magsaysay Lozada; Vidhu Aggarwal & Petra Kuppers; Neela Banerjee + Beau Sia, Faisal Mohyuddin, Janine Lim, Kirin Khan, Lawrence-Minh Bùi Davis, Mimi Khúc, Nayomi Munaweera, Ramy El-Etreby (constellations!), Taz Ahmed & traci kato-kiriyama.

Much love to TDS & TDS grinds: Butch Schwarzkopf, Christian Aldana, Czaerra Galicinao Ucol, David Maduli, Eunice Andrada, Janice Lobo Sapigao, Keana Aguila Labra, Liaa Melissa Fernandez, Maria Bolaños, Michelle Peñaloza, Rachelle Cruz, with a shoutout to everyone involved in the epic months of the festival & TULA for Typhoon Relief; to CBAW: especially Seema, Ali Husain, Amelia Bane, Ashy Palliparambil, Ben Weakley, Joe Merritt, We Were Not Alone crew, Rob Haney; all the Day of Belonging participants and presenters; to BIPOC Writing Community: Faith Adiele & Serena W. Lin for the gathering vision; fellow participants Arthur Kayzakian, Caroline M. Mar, Faria Ali, Miguel Angel Angeles, Raychelle Heath & Tara Sarath, for deep ongoing care. Some events change your DNA: Francis Arevalo (The Walk), Desirée Dawson, & Kimmortal, with big thanks to Johnny D Trinh for collaborations since; the channeling circle for Holly: Niki, Kim, Tin, Jay & Julz; Crips for eSims for Gaza: Jane Shi, Leah Lakshmi Piepzna-Samarasinha & Alice Wong, Maria for splitting labour with me, all the other volunteers, and most of all Palestinian folks on the ground sharing survival with each other.

∽

For *Tabako on the Windowill*: Chris Abani, what a gift: E'seun o! Your eyes, your mode of attention brought this into its full being. Thank you enough? Can never. Selina Boan, Kaie Kellough, and Truong Tran—thank you for such beautiful and insightful notes about this work, for truly reading its vision. Alayna Munce and Manahil Bandukwala, so much growth in our back-and-forths: thank you for your deep care in the production process. Kilby Smith-McGregor for such a stunning cover and book design. Word to Dani Alcalde-Sidloski & Harri Pratt, to Cynthia Dewi Oka, David Maduli, Phanuel Antwi, Rup Sidhu, and and and Mahal Julay. Carlo Sayo, who saw the author photo just standing there. Word to so much. Word to Denise. Word to Xtina & Jamie ;) Brenda Leifso and everyone at Brick Books—word to Nick Thran and all the acquisitions team—for giving this book a home and bringing it to the world.

Early readers whose witnessing, notes, and collab sessions helped me build towards this book: Aliyah Muhammad, Rachelle Cruz, Jason "let's build" Magabo Perez, KC Lehman, and Tara Sarath. Seema Reza who literally called me to put the manuscript together. Preeti Dhaliwal & Ruby Singh for allowing me to learn from working with you and nourishing back my work in our processes (and messages). Junie Désil: oceans & islands. Arthur Kayzakian & Karla Cordero: inspiration strikes. Adrian Matejka, Aurora Masum-Javed, Chris Gatchalian and Shaan Amin: y'all read a different project altogether, but the sharpening translates. Keana Aguila Labra & Maria Bolaños for that interview. Maria, b-roll ongoing, and that map! Kevin Dublin & Anthony Fangary for late night revisions. Faisal Mohyuddin: chal. Cynthia: the questions, the journey; David: the sessions, the sessions. The check-ins on each other, the deepening beneath them.

❧

Love to everyone—near & far, directly & indirectly—involved in the ongoing honouring of those we carry. For Eric DJ Wundrkut (Forever) Cardeno and Holly DJ Holla Holly Kang. For Kat Zu'comulwat Norris, the poetry in every aspect of your being. Abby. Babu Uncle. Andy. Chris. Dags. Evangelista. Everlinda Silva: Tita Bay. Io. Justin. Leila. Margie. Neelam. Nenix. Patricia. Qayyum. Spencer. Valaurie. For these stolen unceded lands right here. For those who best love the lands of my blood and birth. For those who've cared and care for any land that's blessed my feet. For Congo. For Sudan. For Palestine. Say Noura, Ayla, Suhaib, Lana, Malek, Amr, Khadija, Ahmed, Rital, Ghadir, & Lama. More than a thousand names in each: may every lost name return through the birth of a new life, and free. How we carry and are carried by those we choose—and have no choice but—to grieve: it's in everything.

For our next generations, all my nieces & nephews on the Subcontinent & the Arkipelago, and: Aikulola, Ali, Alva, Amélie, Anaiya, Apollo, Aria, Arvin, Avnika, Bonnie, Briggs, Cal, Camilo, Devon, Eli, Emiko, Eva, Everly, Finn, G-4, Honey Rose, Iliana, Imaan, Isaac, Isana, Isley, Isobel, Jovan, Kabir, Kai, Kailash, Kalani, Kalayaan, Kaleo, Kanoa, Kawayan, Kiera, Kylen, Leila, Leo, Liam, Loïc, Luke, Luna, Malia, Maren, Maya, Mia, Mya, Naviya, Nikhil, Nima, Norrin, Omar, Paul, Phoenix, Phoenix,

Poet, Prince, Raiden, Ria, Rielle, Rohan, Roman, Sasha, Sienna, Silver, Siyana, Sunum, Witton, Xyriez, Zach, Zayan, Zuleihka, & beyond—

Full circle: Julay & Tala. Fe, Krishna, & Rina. Lineages to get to you and reach. Whatever else this life is, it's also beautiful.

If you're still reading: Salamat. Shukriyah. [Unreadable Orasyon.]

∽

Wonder cuts the keys to doors between the worlds.

Ingat,

—Hari Alluri

Photo credit: Carlo Sayo

HARI ALLURI (he/him/siya) is an uninvited migrant poet of Philippine and South Indian descent who lives, writes, and works on unceded Coast Salish territories of the Musqueam, Squamish and Tsleil-Waututh peoples, and Ts'uubaa-asatx lands of Hul'q'umi'num-speaking peoples. Author of *The Flayed City* (Kaya Press), *carving ashes* (CiCAC/Thompson Rivers Press), and chapbooks *Our Echo of Sudden Mercy* (Next Page Press) and *The Promise of Rust* (Mouthfeel Press), siya is a recipient of the Vera Manuel Award for Poetry and grants from the BC Arts Council, Canada Council of the Arts, and National Film Board of Canada, among other prizes, grants, fellowships and residencies.

Printed by Imprimerie Gauvin
Gatineau, Québec